THE ROOKIE TRADING SYSTEMS

THE ONLY TRADING SYSTEMS YOU WILL EVER NEED TO PURCHASE TO BECOME A SUCCESFUL TRADER

A STRAIGHT TO THE POINT NO WAFFLE GUIDE TO TRADING USING TRIED AND TESTED TRADING SYSTEMS

Author Warren Rozen 2021

INTRODUCTION

Hi,

Thank you for purchasing the FOUR tried and tested trading systems. Before getting on with the serious business of how to operate these straight forward trading strategies let me get one thing clear in your mind.

Trading is a very risky business, we will eliminate some of the risk by placing stop losses on our trades and by using clear sensible tried and tested strategies, but even armed with this information it is possible to lose **some,** if not **all** of your betting bank.

The biggest obstacle you must overcome when trading is yourself. Whilst I will endeavour to highlight some of the pitfalls you are likely to encounter, at the end of the day it is yourself against the market.

If the market moves against you are you the type of person to panic and pull out of a potential winning trade? Will you try to chase losses? If you have never bet before any number of negative traits may show themselves, using good money management techniques and only playing the markets when you have good reason to do so should help to eliminate some of the risks, but not the bad habits.

It is for this reason initially I recommend you trade using a Demo account. Most trading platforms have this type of account and the platform I am going to recommend to you has a demo trading platform. Use this until you are confident enough to start trading live. How will you know when to switch to a live account? Only when you have proven to yourself that you have what it takes and you are making steady regular profits.

When switching to the live account only deposit money you are prepared to lose and have no other use for than to gamble with. It is an unfortunate phrase (to gamble) but we are playing the financial markets (market being the operative word here) markets move up and down and are difficult to predict. With hindsight we would all be millionaires and unfortunately hindsight is a gift no one possesses and cannot be taught.

I cannot be held personally responsible for any losses you incur trading, I can only advise you on the size of bank required and reminding you here before you commence, that it is possible to lose your bank if betting irrationally or irresponsibly and not adhering to the rules set out in this manual.

CONTENTS

LOSING IS PART OF WINNING 05

WINNING TRADES VERSUS LOSING TRADES 06

GETTING STARTED 08

THE SYSTEMS 10

IPLEMENTING THE FOUR SYSTEMS 12
    THE SINGLE CROSSOVER 12
    THE DOUBLE CROSSOVER 13
    MOVING AVERAGE CROSSOVERS 14

MARKET BREAKOUT SYSTEM 16
    THE DONCHIAN TREND SYSTEM 16
    PLOTTING POSSIBLE TURNING POINTS 16

BOLLINGER BREAKOUT SYSTEM 20
    PLACING TRADES 22
    STOP LOSSES 22
    MARGINS 23

MONEY MANAGEMENT 24

RISK AND REWARD 27

LOSING IS PART OF WINNING

When I started out trading if someone had told me that to be a good trader I would have to accept losses and possible losing runs would I have had second thoughts? No not at all. In fact having been a semi professional gambler on the horses I know that this is all part and parcel of the business. No one wins all of the time, this is impossible. The hardest times are riding the inevitable losing runs. What you have to consider is if the profit from your winning runs cover the losses from the losing runs, that's fine. But if it is the other way around then stop and have a good look at your strategy and try to find out why it is failing. If you cannot put your finger on the reason then don't give up your day job.

WINNING TRADES VERSUS LOSING TRADES

Below is a trading account supplied by a professional trader on the Cocoa Market, note: initially that there were 17 losing trades in a row. His belief in the strategy enabled him to put these losing runs behind him and press on knowing a big winning trade was about to happen.

	Unit	Entry	Position	Price	Quant	Exit	%	Profit	Total
1	1	27 Apr	L	2,249	6	2,234	(2.4)	($1,197)	
2	1	6 May	L L	2,261	6	2,246	(2.1)	($1.026)	
3	1	12 May	L L	2,276	6	2,261	(2.2)	($1.036)	
4	1	14 May	L L	2,283	6	2,268	(2.4)	($1.133)	
5	1	23 Jun	S	2,100	6	2,114	(2.3)	($1.061)	
6	1	25 Jun	S	2,094	6	2,108	(2.4)	($1.053)	
7	1	29 Jun	S	2,085	6	2,099	(3.0)	($1.317)	
8	1	15 Jul	S	2,070	6	2,084	(2.5)	($1,066)	
9	1	27 Jul	S	2,069	5	2,083	(1.9)	($ 777)	
10	1	3 Aug	S	2,050	5	2,064	(2.7)	($1.104)	
11	1	13 Aug	S	2,036	6	2,049	(2.2)	($ 848)	

12	1	17 Aug	S	2,024	6	2,036	(3.0)	($1,155)	
13	1	24 Aug	S	2,024	6	2,035	(2.4)	($ 874)	
14	1	16 Sep	S	2,014	5	2,026	(2.2)	($ 756)	
15	1	1 Oct	S	1,979	5	1,992	(2.1)	($ 845)	
16	1	13 Oct	S	1,976	5	1,988	(2.4)	($ 779)	
17	1	28 Oct	S	1,967	5	1,979	(2.1)	($ 722)	($16,750)
18	1	6 Nov	S	1,961	5	1,438	75.0	$24,940	
19	2	20 Nov	S	1,918	6	1,928	(2.4)	($ 799)	
20	2	24 Nov	S	1,903	6	1,914	(3.0)	($ 975)	
21	2	30 Nov	S	1,982	5	1,903	(2.7)	($ 834)	
22	2	8 Dec	S	1,873	5	1,438	67.2	$20,575	
23	3	21 Dec	S	1,824	5	1,836	(3.5)	($1,075)	
24	3	4 Jan	S	1,808	5	1,820	(2.4)	($ 709)	
25	3	15 Jan	S	1,798	4	1,438	46.7	$13,468	
26	4	25 Jan	S	1,748	4	1,760	(2.1)	($ 608)	
27	4	27 Jan	S	1,742	4	1,754	(2.1)	($ 605)	
28	4	8 Feb	S	1,738	7	1,438	42.8	$19,275	$55,903

As you can see from the above although the winning trades were just 4 from 28 (14%) if you strategy is sound then it's the bottom line that counts in this case a $55,903 profit.

GETTING STARTED

As a beginner I recommend you open an account with the easiest trading platform to use, most are easy to navigate these days. Look for a site that is easy to navigate around and the charts are simple to set up. I always enquired about setting up a deal for new traders. One site I used gave the following deal. If you deposit $75 into your account it would match this amount giving you a total of $150 to get started which is quite possible if betting to $2 (the minimum stake)

Once you have given them the required details you are ready to get started. Don't forget to open up a demo or practice account too, this is the best way to test any strategy without losing money. Highly recommended to kick off your trading education.

Before I get into explaining the four trading systems, any trader worth his salt keeps up to date with financial news and announcements. I like to watch Bloomberg TV on the satellite news channel, you can always keep up to date online at www.bloomberg.com this is a site I thoroughly recommend as it has educational videos, all the latest news and trading advices. I am an avid fan of the morning call programme, on just before the Asian markets open at midnight and spend a lot watching this program well into the small hours of the morning. Recent advices that prompted me to trade was advice that Oil would rise at the time it was sat on $40 a barrel and rose to over $60 and is even higher at the time of writing this. I made over $4k to a $3 stake backing this market to go up. Other recent advices were The Dow Jones and S&P markets to rise again making me $2K to again $3 stakes on each market. Also you need to keep up to date with the latest financial announcements which will include interest rates, jobless figures, retail profits etc. My favoured site is www.dailyfx.com

When entering the site you will bring up all of the forthcoming announcements for the week, the ones to note are the **HIGH** which are likely to move the markets. The one announcement that must be avoided (try to close off all open trades around this announcement) is the US jobless figures, the Non farm payroll which comes out on the first Friday of every month bang on 1.30

Below is a screenshot of announcements to come on, note High are likely to come from the USA or GB

Circled and arrowed and are the **KEY** announcements likely to move the markets to any significant extent.

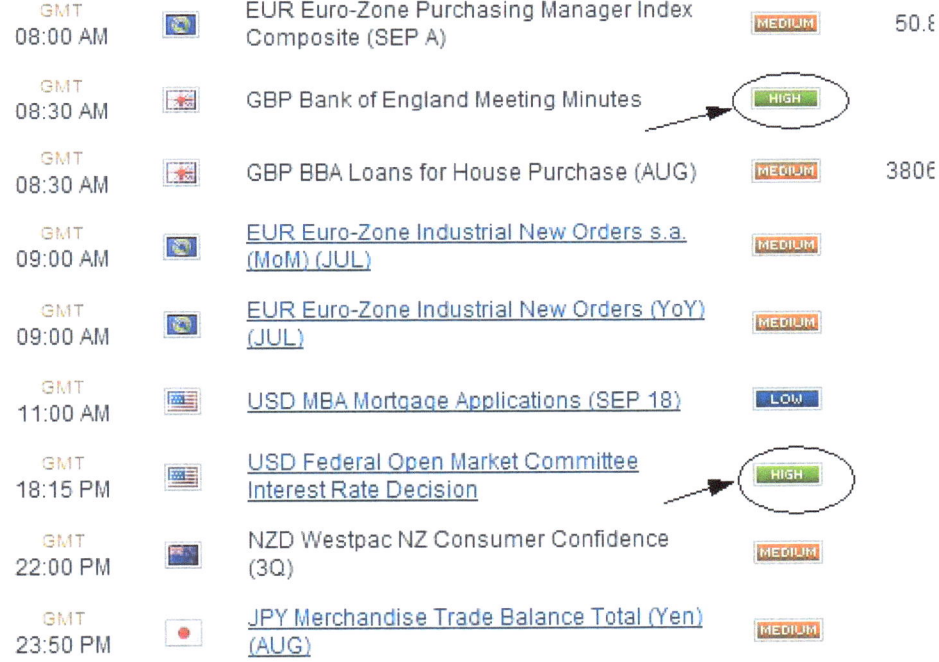

For the sake of a few minutes each day it will pay to keep up with this information.

THE SYSTEMS

We are now going to take a look at the systems I am recommending to you to get you started on the road to successful trading.

The markets to trade in will eventually be your own choice of course BUT to start with I recommend you use the slower moving markets firstly on the Demo account and then live. I trade most of the major currency markets which are a little more volatile than the indices such as the Footsie or Dax.

The markets I recommend you should get a feel for initially are the FTSE Rolling Daily, DAX 30 Rolling daily (note this market tends to follow the Footsie) and the one Currency market the USD / JPY Rolling Daily

Plenty to be getting on with to start with, it is advisable that with all markets you trade, but firstly you need to check the long term trend for that market. After the recent global financial crash it is safe to say that most markets are recovering and shares are on the up, but you need to check the currency markets to see which currency is strongest.

To do this, go into one of the trading charts on the homepage of the site

Circled is the market of interest then click on the chart symbol to bring up the trading chart.

Below is the chart showing how to set up indicators highlighting medium to long term trends in the USD/JPY market

THE ROOKIE TRADING SYSTEMS

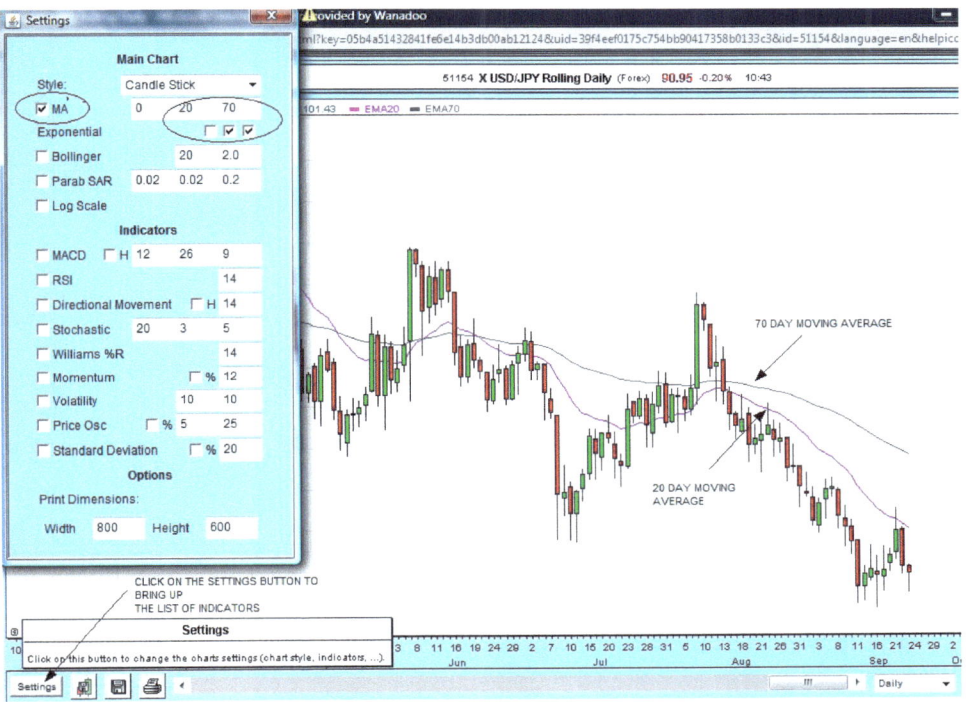

Note: Clicking on settings will bring up the indicator box. Tick the MA (moving average) box. Type in 20 and 70 and click the exponential box.

You will note these lines have been plotted on the candle chart, the grey line the 70 day MA and the pink line the 20 day MA. It is clear that in this market there is a down trend as the 20 day moving average (the quicker moving of the two) crosses the 70 in Mid June and the market has moved down since, apart from the peak early August.

The significance for you as a trader is that the bigger percentage of your trades are going to be short (sell trades) in the above market. Knowing the trend is a must and will be explained in more detail later.

IMPLEMENTING THE FOUR SYSTEMS

It is now time to get into the nuts and bolts of the trading systems, starting with the most simple.

THE SINGLE CROSSOVER

Go to the homepage and click on the FTSE Rolling Daily Chart

Click on the 20 EMA and the 50 EMA and save these settings

Below is an example of a sell signal the system on the FTSE 100 from January 2008 to mid July 2009

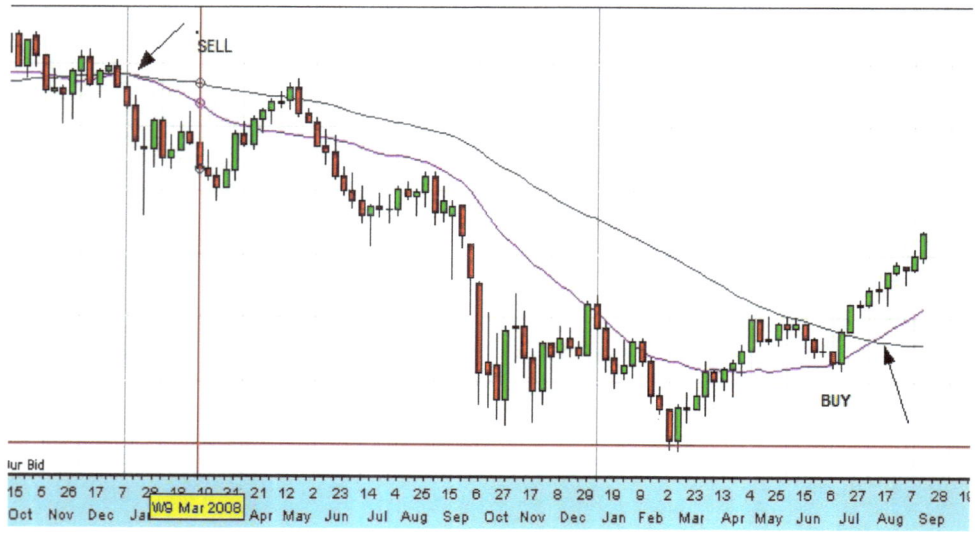

Note: The arrow top left indicates when we would have placed a sell bet on the market at 6410 we would have exited the market at 4315 plus at +2095 points profit. Then bought at the 4315 point (15/7/09) the market currently stands at 5170 (17/9/2009) +855 points + 2950 in just 7 months trading a single market.

The system is a simple way of recognising the trend we use two exponential moving averages the 20 and the 50. Note that in the bottom right hand corner the chart must be set to **daily**

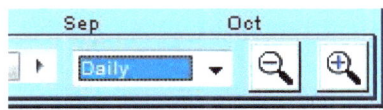

The basis of the system is quite simple when the quicker moving average crosses the slower moving average in the example above cutting through initially downward. Then at this point you go short in the market (sell) and you keep this position open until the quicker moving average cuts back through the slower moving back up. Once this occurs then we switch to a long position (buy)

The idea is that you are continually trading, you are in long or short positions all of the time. As you can see, trades can last weeks, months or in some cases even years. One market can be traded in this manner or multiple markets depending on the size of your bank. No stop losses were used by the traders using this system (I will go into stops in the money management part of the system) which I find amazing.

As you can see from January 2008 through to July 2009 it was possible to make nearly 3000 pips (points) from this one market alone. I suggest you plot these moving averages on several markets to get a feel for how the markets move.

THE DOUBLE CROSSOVER

Again we are using the 20-50 EMA but adding an even faster moving average. The 5 EMA on your settings you need to plot the 5-20 and 50 exponential moving averages as below

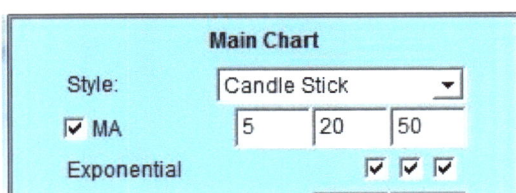

The 5 EMA is added to the chart in this strategy and the other settings remain unchanged. The 5 EMA is added to catch upward or downward movement more quickly than the single crossover strategy. You are more likely to be in and out of trades on a shorter time scale, but the theory remains the same. Whilst the 5 is above the 20 and both above the 50 you are trading long, if they remain below you are trading short

MOVING AVERAGE CROSSOVERS

Below is a good example of the type of crossover we are looking for

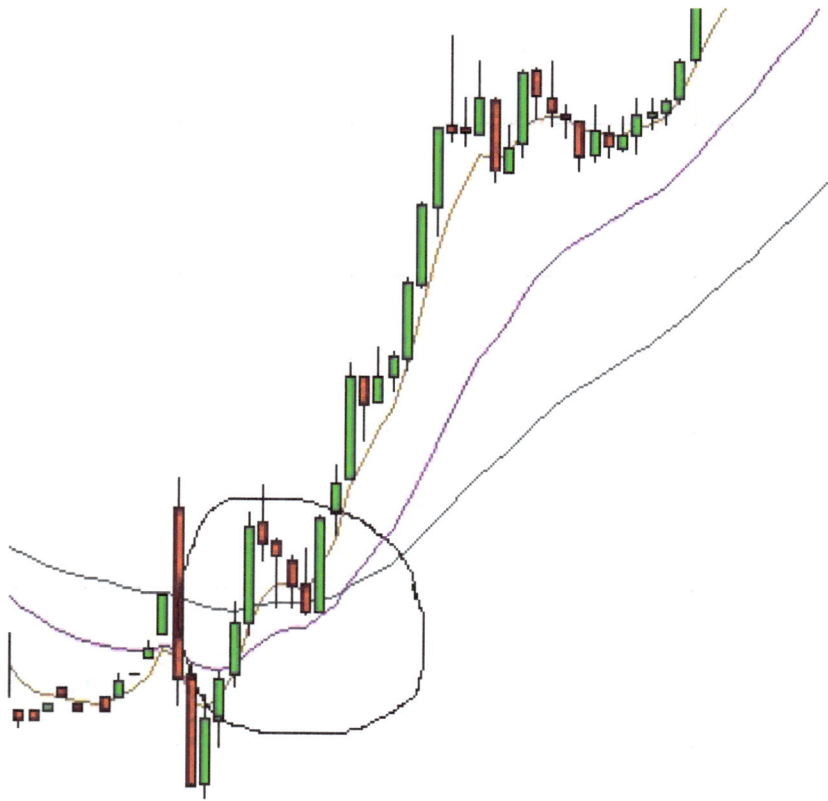

Note: I have circled the point where the three moving averages cross

1/ the 5EMA (orange) crosses the 20EMA (pink) they both cross the 50EMA (grey) in an upward direction. The angle of the 5EMA is important the steeper the rise or fall is a good pointer to how strong the trade may be. In this case the market rose all day.

The example is an indication of how a flat market where the EMA's are up and down in a shallow pattern then all of a sudden take off to make another strong trade of 100+ points

MARKET BREAKOUT SYSTEM

THE DONCHIAN TREND SYSTEM

I believe that this method of trading is all that you really need to make money as it is based upon the true fundamentals of trading. I mentioned in the marketing information that I would teach you how to profit from the psychology of other traders. This method will show you to do this and make you realise what trading is all about.

Basically a market tends to move within support and resistance lines. It may move up and down bouncing off the same support and resistance for days, weeks, months or even years in flat sideways moving markets. I think we are about to enter one of these phases after the recent shocks in the banking sector where risk has been put on the back burner for the time being.

There is nothing wrong with flat market that consistently hits the previous highs and lows when the markets become predictable. Small profits may be made buying and selling within these narrow channels of activity. But to really hit the big time from market volatility is when a market **breaks out** from these set channels of activity. It is here you need to be on the button and buy into the breakout.

The previous support or resistance may be left well behind as the market pushes higher or lower, and this new direction as stated could be short lived or last for quite some time. Previous resistance to a market may now become support or visa versa.

PLOTTING POSSIBLE TURNING POINTS

I mentioned in the marketing info about plotting random lines on a piece of paper that had no significance to any market, but when laid on top of any market a case could be made for the existence of each line. Well the lines you are going to plot are very significant and are plotted by all professional traders and act as key support and resistance points where the markets are likely to break out.

At the end of each trading week chose any market and look at the previous 20 days activity. The key points for us are the highest high of the previous 20 days and the lowest low of the previous 20 days.

To apply these lines go to the hourly chart. The new trading week as I am typing this was week commencing the 21st of September 2009 so the previous 20 days trading in this case is the 24th of August through to the 21st of September (note weekends are not included as the markets close on a Friday evening)

On the hourly chart you need to note the highest high over this period and the lowest low. Draw the lines on the chart for the coming week onto your chosen market.

You also need to draw the lines for the highest high of the past 55 days trading and the lowest low. Or at least note these highs and lows as they may not be visible on the hourly chart. This period would go back to the 6th of July 2009 (again no weekends included)

On the FTSE Rolling daily the 55 day high was 5200 the same as the 20 day high, a very significant turning point.

The 55 day low was 4093 and the 20 day low was 4772

The example below shows the lines plotted on the **daily** chart

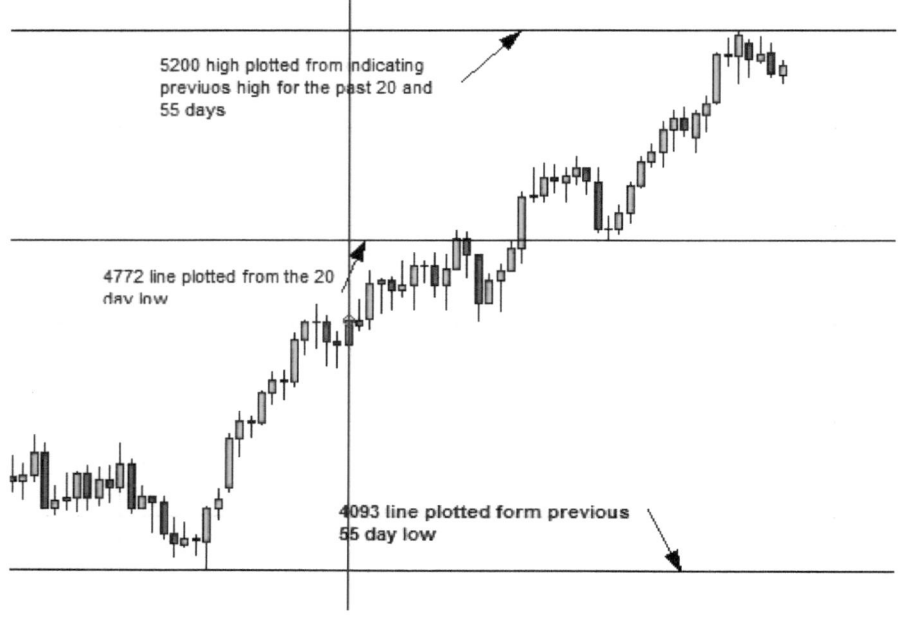

The market hit the 20 and 55 day high on the 18th of September and we started the new trading week on the 20th of September. Moving to a lower time scale on the charts (hourly) we can clearly see that on the 18th, the Market had tested the 5200 on three occasions making this line a solid resistance point. Being confident the market cannot move higher it would make perfect sense now to place a short trade (sell) for the coming week

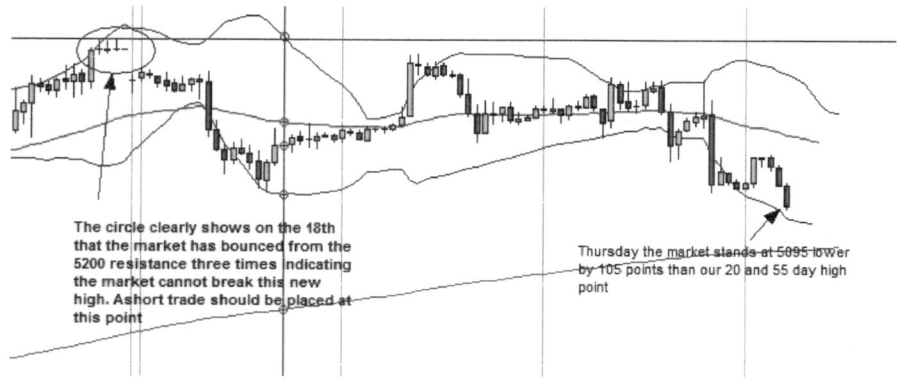

It would be possible for the market to move right back down to the previous 20 day low of 4772 or even to the 55day low of 4093.

The main factor here is that we knew where the new support or resistance level was for the coming week and have profited from this knowledge. Another significant factor here is that the new resistance was formed on a 00 line (5200) which is another strong psychological barrier in a trader's mindset. **NOTE double zero lines are very significant support and resistant area's**

It is around these lines that you may encounter extra volatility as traders cannot make up their minds as to whether the market will break higher at or rebound. Make sure that you are clear in your own mind that the volatility has ended and wait to see if the market has broken out above our plotted support and resistance or failed and bounced off. In this case switching back to the hourly chart from the weekly, it was clear as the candles had three attempts to push up and that a short trade was clearly the sensible and only option.

Note that Support and Resistance areas are the battle grounds where both buyers and sellers converge with the market break and reach new highs? Buyers when the market pushes up, sellers win the market rebounds. Wait until the market has made up its mind before buying or selling at these points.

BOLLINGER BREAKOUT SYSTEM

I really like using Bollinger bands as an overbought or oversold indicator for the market. This simple system can be used for long or short term trades on all markets.

The system the traders used were long term but my own easy footsie system uses the same strategy on the 5 minute chart Below is an example of the system on the daily chart

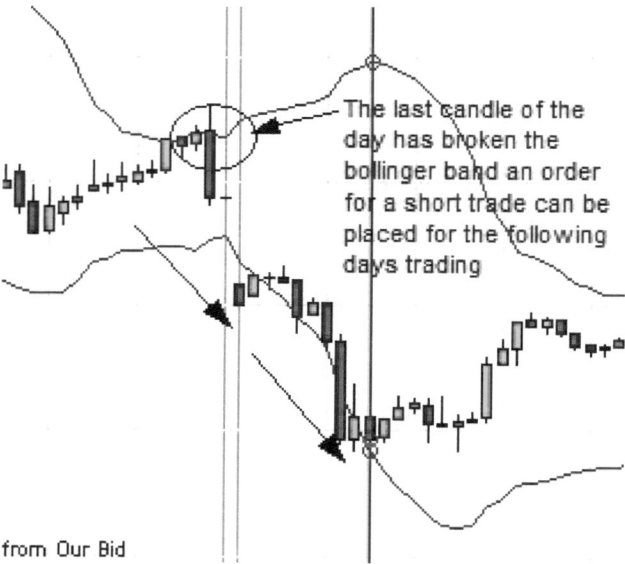

The basis of the system is to browse the markets looking for one where the Bollinger Band has been broken by the last candle to form on any given trading day (clearly indicated above) in this case the market was overbought as the top Bollinger band has been broken. The following day the market dropped and continued on its downward path for over 200 pips. A short order was placed after the market had closed that evening, this way you can go to bed and forget about having to be around when the market opens the following day.

No limit was placed on the profit but a stop loss was placed 50 points above the top of the last candle.

Below is an example of a buy trade on the hourly chart where the market is oversold as the market has penetrated the bottom Bollinger. At this point a buy trade can be placed. Watch the market until the candles break through the top band then close off the trade taking the profit, in this case the market being the Footsie 100 bought at 4963 and closed out at 5033 a nice little 70 pip trade.

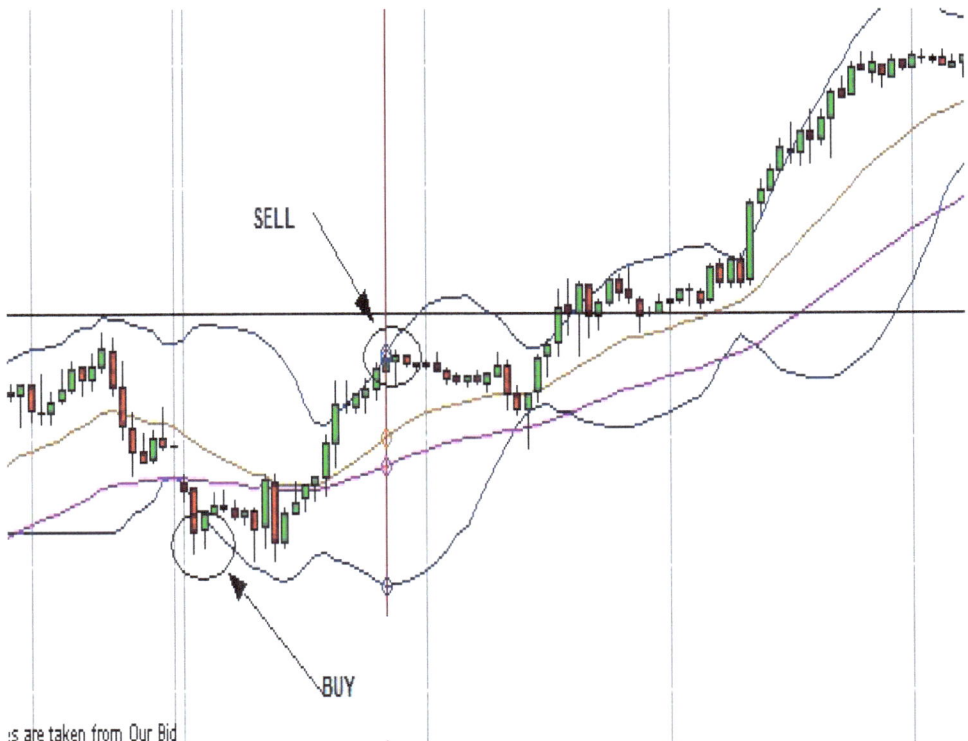

Note the spikes at the bottom of the of the candles again are good indication the market has tried to push down and failed again

I did not have to look too far for this example as it is regular occurrence in ALL markets and a very good strategy long or short term.

PLACING TRADES

I am not going to write reams of pages on how to place a trade, you need to go to the trading platform you have decided to open an account with and use the demo account to get used to using their site before placing real trades with real money.

STOP LOSSES

Again how to place stops will be explained on most sites in the trading workshops but you need to know the levels I recommend for each system. The trading rookies never risked more than 2% of their bank on each trade.

Short Term trades.

Trades you expect to last no more than an hour or so should be placed using a 20 point stop loss.

Medium term trades.

Trades lasting just one day up to two to three days should be placed using a 50 point stop loss.

Long term Trades.

Longer term trades i.e. trades lasting over a three day period possible stretching into weeks or even months should be placed using at least a 100 point stop loss.

Note: a good strategy with longer term trades is to move your stop loss as the market moves up or down. If you keep your stop 100 points behind the market then at some stage you should be in a break even position if the market has moved 100 points in your favour and you are sat 100 points behind with your stop then at this stage if you keep the stop in this position you cannot lose.

Going back to the size of bank required and risking only 2% means you must be able to cover your stop and margin

MARGINS

Scenario 1

You have exactly £300 in your account

In the case of the FTSE, the minimum margin is 30 and the maximum computer generated stop-loss is 150. This is the maximum in margin it will hold for a £1 position. So with the trade example above, the minimum margin required, which you must have in your Tradefair Spreads account is 30 x 10 = £300 and because you are 'buying' the FTSE, the stop-loss would be placed 24 points below your entry price

(80% of the margin - it's 80% to help prevent your account going into a negative balance).

Scenario 2

You have £10,000 in your account and are placing the same trade

In this case, the Tradefair Spreads platform will take the maximum amount of margin required (150) and place the automatic stop-loss 120 points below your entry price (80% of the margin). If the market falls 120 points, your trade will be stopped automatically and on this occasion you would have lost £1,200. The stop loss was placed 120 points away because this is 80% of the maximum computer generated stop

MONEY MANAGEMENT

To win in any form of betting you must have self control. If you are experiencing a losing run then it is very easy to lose all sense of self control and start to chase losses. A good money management system means nothing if you cannot be disciplined and walk away form losing trades and not chase losses.

Money management should be kept very simple indeed, I have a bank of X amount of pounds and as mentioned above place just 2% of the bank on each bet that I place. When the bank increases then you can start to increase your stakes.

Just say for instance you have deposited $500 into your account and you are starting to bet with minimum stakes of $2. If you double your bank to $1000 you are showing all the right signs of becoming a successful trader and you should consider increasing your stakes at this point. The sensible option would be to double your stakes. I prefer to take a slower route as I believe one day trading to $2 and then all of a sudden the following day you are playing with double those stakes, can and will affect your judgement. Increase your stakes to just $3. This small increase should not affect your judgement as much and all the time your bank is getting further from going bust if you make a few losing trades.

There is a saying that scared money never wins and this is true. Sailing too close to the wind with your stakes and bank, increases tension, causes bad judgment and ultimately will cause you to fail.

Big bank, small stakes and a sound strategy means long term you are going to win.

The friend I mentioned in the marketing info has kindly copied me his recent trading activity. He started trading with the £75 deposit and £75 tradefair placed in his account. His stakes should have been £3 when he hit the £300, mark £4 when he hit the £600 and so on. As you can see although he has done a great job of reading and interpreting the system making a fantastic profit, he is showing an undisciplined approach to money management that may eventually be his downfall. His bigger staked trades are in his own words "chasing losses" a trait he cannot seem to shake off.

ALL £2 trades highlighted in blue.

Below is an extract from Steve James trading account who started trading at the beginning of July with just £150 in his trading account

20-Jul-09	10:09	Trade (3.00) Buy X GBP/USD Rolling Daily of 1.6507		60	729.19	GBP
20-Jul-09	11:48	Trade (5.00) Buy X GBP/USD Rolling Daily of 1.6525		100	629.19	GBP
20-Jul-09	16:03	Trade (4.00) Buy FTSE Rolling Daily of 4440.0		40	589.19	GBP
22-Jul-09	08:33	Trade (2) Buy X EUR/USD Rolling Daily of 1.4175	48		637.19	GBP
24-Jul-09	09:13	Trade (3.00) Buy FTSE Rolling Daily of 4590.0		60	577.19	GBP
24-Jul-09	14:02	Trade (5) Buy FTSE Rolling Daily of 4580.0	59		636.19	GBP
28-Jul-09	10:01	Trade (2) Sell X USD/CHF Rolling Daily of 1.0675	12		648.19	GBP
30-Jul-09	21:16	Trade (7447228) Buy 2.00 of Wall Street Rolling Daily		0.63	647.56	GBP
30-Jul-09	21:16	Trade (7447235) Buy 2.00 of S&P Rolling Daily		0.68	646.88	GBP
31-Jul-09	21:16	Trade (7447228) Buy 2.00 of Wall Street Rolling Daily		1.88	645	GBP
31-Jul-09	21:16	Trade (7447235) Buy 2.00 of S&P Rolling Daily		2.02	642.98	GBP
03-Aug-09	21:20	Trade (7447228) Buy 2.00 of Wall Street Rolling Daily		0.64	642.34	GBP
03-Aug-09	21:20	Trade (7447235) Buy 2.00 of S&P Rolling Daily		0.69	641.65	GBP
04-Aug-09	21:17	Trade (7447228) Buy 2.00 of Wall Street Rolling Daily		0.64	641.01	GBP
04-Aug-09	21:17	Trade (7447228) Buy 2.00 of Wall Street Rolling Daily	9.01		650.02	GBP
04-Aug-09	21:17	Trade (7447235) Buy 2.00 of S&P Rolling Daily		0.69	649.33	GBP
05-Aug-09	12:19	Trade (2) Sell S&P Rolling Daily of 1007.1	478		1127.33	GBP
05-Aug-09	12:19	Trade (2) Sell Wall Street Rolling Daily of 9320	378		1505.33	GBP
06-Aug-09	11:01	Trade (2) Buy X USD/JPY Rolling Daily of 95.36	6		1511.33	GBP

THE ROOKIE TRADING SYSTEMS

Date	Time	Trade			Balance	Currency
07-Aug-09	11:40	Trade (2) Buy FTSE Rolling Daily of 4636.3	3.4		1514.73	GBP
11-Aug-09	10:25	Trade (2) Buy FTSE Rolling Daily of 4729.3	20.4		1535.13	GBP
13-Aug-09	02:50	Trade (5.00) Sell X USD/JPY Rolling Daily of 95.85		150	1385.13	GBP
13-Aug-09	13:31	Trade (5) Buy FTSE Rolling Daily of 4764.3	96		1481.13	GBP
14-Aug-09	08:17	Trade (2) Buy X USD/JPY Rolling Daily of 95.13	26		1507.13	GBP
25-Aug-09	21:16	Trade (7591001) Buy 2.00 of X AUD/NZD Rolling Daily		0.33	1506.8	GBP
26-Aug-09	07:00	Trade (2.00) Sell X AUD/NZD Rolling Daily of 1.2162		118	1388.8	GBP
26-Aug-09	14:14	Trade (5) Buy FTSE Rolling Daily of 4896.3	42.5		1431.3	GBP
27-Aug-09	08:10	Trade (2.00) Buy X GBP/USD Rolling Daily of 1.6223		40	1391.3	GBP
27-Aug-09	10:25	Trade (4) Buy X GBP/USD Rolling Daily of 1.6200	72		1463.3	GBP
27-Aug-09	13:35	Trade (2) Buy X GBP/USD Rolling Daily of 1.6200	24		1487.3	GBP
28-Aug-09	08:05	Trade (3) Buy FTSE Rolling Daily of 4903.5	15.9		1503.2	GBP
28-Aug-09	14:04	Trade (3.00) Buy FTSE Rolling Daily of 4935.3		60	1443.2	GBP
28-Aug-09	21:17	Trade (7616925) Sell 5.00 of FTSE Rolling Daily		1.01	1442.19	GBP
31-Aug-09	10:28	Trade (5) Buy FTSE Rolling Daily of 4886.5	136.5		1578.69	GBP
01-Sep-09	08:07	Trade (2.00) Buy X GBP/USD Rolling Daily of 1.6355		40	1538.69	GBP
01-Sep-09	09:57	Trade (2) Buy X GBP/USD Rolling Daily of 1.6254	220		1758.69	GBP
02-Sep-09	08:53	Trade (2) Buy X USD/JPY Rolling Daily of 92.76	42		1800.69	GBP
03-Sep-09	12:19	Trade (2.00) Buy X EUR/USD Rolling Daily of 1.4321		40	1760.69	GBP
03-Sep-09	12:44	Trade (4.00) Buy X EUR/USD Rolling Daily of 1.4348		88	1672.69	GBP
03-Sep-09	13:39	Trade (5) Buy X EUR/USD Rolling Daily of 1.4304	165		1837.69	GBP
04-Sep-09	12:58	Trade (2) Buy X EUR/USD Rolling Daily of 1.4261	24		1861.69	GBP
07-Sep-09	08:58	Trade (1.00) Buy FTSE Rolling Daily of 4907.0		20	1841.69	GBP
07-Sep-09	21:17	Trade (7652135) Sell 4.00 of FTSE Rolling Daily		0.27	1841.42	GBP

RISK REWARD

We have already established that trading is a risky business. Before entering into a trade realistically if the trade goes your way then you should be measuring the capital you are risking versus the likely reward for taking on this risk i.e. potential profits.

As I have also stated markets cannot be 100% accurately predicted. What looks like a solid trade could easily turn against you for no apparent reason there are so many unknown that can affect a trade and turn it around. We have to have confidence that when the bet is placed we have a very good reason to place it and an idea of where the trade is likely to finish.

Going back to our strategies, if placing a trade using Donchian system placing a sell trade at the 20 day high of 5200 could possibly see a long term gain of 428 pips if the market came back down to the 20 day low of 4772 and in this case justifies placing a bet with a 50 point stop loss.

If using the Bollinger breakout system and the candle had broken the highest band at 5200 but the bottom band was just 20 points away at 5480, then placing a trade with a 50 point stop to gain just 20 points profit would be madness. In a case like this the risk is not worth the reward.

Basically what I am saying here is that we don't really know where the market will run out of steam but we have an idea. If the reward is greater than the risk then a bet should be placed, if not wait for clearer opportunities.

Best of Luck in Trading Warren Rozen

www.ingramcontent.com/pod-product-compliance
Lightning Source LLC
Chambersburg PA
CBHW040358220526
45473CB00021B/2826